Elevate Your Life:
The 7 Core Principles of Success

A Journey to Unleash Your Potential and Achieve Extraordinary Success

Tony Oloko

Copyright © 2012 Tony Oloko

All rights reserved.

ISBN: 9798857060353

The 7 Core Principles of Success

DEDICATION

To all those who believe in the power of growth, connection, and the pursuit of their dreams. May the principles within these pages inspire you to elevate your life, embrace your potential, and create a lasting impact on the world. This book is dedicated to your journey of success and fulfillment.

Table of Contents

Acknowledgements	9
Introduction	10
Why These 7 Core Principles?	10
Your Path to Elevate Your Life	13
Chapter 1: The Principle of Clarity	14
Discovering Your Purpose	14
Defining Your Vision	15
Aligning Actions with Values	16
Cultivating Focus and Direction	17
Embracing the Path of Exploration	18
Overcoming Obstacles and Doubts	19
Celebrating Milestones of Growth	19
Sharing Clarity and Inspiring Others	20
Conclusion Chapter 1.	21
Chapter 2: The Principle of Proactivity	22
Taking Charge of Your Life	22
Embracing Responsibility	23
Navigating Adversity with Resilience	23

Creating Your Own Opportunities	24
Cultivating a Growth Mindset	24
Setting Goals and Taking Action	25
Overcoming Procrastination and Indecision	25
Inspiring Others through Proactivity	26
Embracing Adaptability and Flexibility	26
Building Resilience Through Proactivity	27
Inspiring a Culture of Proactivity	27
Embracing Proactivity as a Lifestyle	28
Proactivity and the Ripple Effect	29
Overcoming Obstacles with Proactivity	29
Cultivating a Proactive Lifestyle	30
Proactivity and Gratitude	30
Conclusion of Chapter 2.	31
Chapter 3: The Principle of Growth Mindset	34
Understanding Fixed vs. Growth Mindset	34
Embracing Challenges as Opportunities	35
The Power of Yet: Turning Failures into Stepping Stones	35

Continuously Improving Yourself	36
Embracing Feedback and Criticism	36
Cultivating Resilience through Mindset	37
Spreading the Seeds of Growth	37
Conclusion of Chapter 3	38
Chapter 4: The Principle of Effective Communication	41
The Art of Active Listening	41
Practicing Empathetic Understanding	42
Assertive Expression for Positive Impact	42
Building Trust and Strong Relationships	43
Conclusion of Chapter 4.	44
Chapter 5: The Principle of Time Management	45
The Value of Time as a Finite Resource	45
Prioritizing Tasks for Maximum Impact	46
Minimizing Distractions and Time Wasters	46
Striking a Work-Life Balance for Well-being	47
Conclusion of Chapter 5.	48

Chapter 6: The Principle of Continuous Learning   50

Embracing a Lifelong Learning Mindset   50

Staying Curious and Adapting to Change   51

Learning from Mistakes and Feedback   51

Innovating and Remaining Relevant   52

Conclusion of Chapter 6.   53

Chapter 7: The Principle of Empathy and Emotional Intelligence   54

The Role of Empathy in Success   54

Understanding and Managing Emotions   55

Nurturing Positive and Supportive Environments   55

Collaboration and Teamwork for Collective Success   56

Conclusion of Chapter 7.   56

Epilogue: A Life Elevated   58

Embracing the Seven Core Principles   61

Reflecting on Your Journey   64

Author's Thank You Message   66

ACKNOWLEDGMENTS

This book would not have been possible without the unwavering support and contributions of many individuals who have guided and inspired me throughout this journey.

I extend my deepest gratitude to my family and friends for their encouragement and belief in my aspirations. Your love and support have been my pillars of strength.

I am indebted to my mentors and advisors whose wisdom and guidance have illuminated my path to understanding and growth.

To the countless individuals who shared their stories, insights, and experiences, thank you for enriching the pages of this book with your wisdom.

Lastly, to the readers, your curiosity and open hearts drive the essence of these words. May this book serve as a source of empowerment and inspiration for your own journey of elevation.

With heartfelt thanks

Introduction

Elevate Your Life: The 7 Core Principles of Success

Welcome to a transformative journey towards personal and professional excellence. In the pages of this book, "Elevate Your Life: The 7 Core Principles of Success," you will embark on a profound exploration of timeless principles that have the power to revolutionize your life.

In a world that moves at lightning speed, it's easy to get caught up in the chaos, lose sight of our aspirations, and settle for mediocrity. However, deep within each one of us lies a reservoir of untapped potential, waiting to be unleashed. This book is a guide to tap into that reservoir and harness the forces that drive success and fulfillment.

Drawing inspiration from the legendary work "The 7 Habits of Highly Effective People," this book aims to empower you with a set of guiding principles that have stood the test of time. These principles are not mere theoretical concepts; they are tried-and-true tools that successful individuals across various fields have utilized to achieve greatness.

Why These 7 Core Principles?

The 7 core principles presented in this book have been carefully selected to address the fundamental aspects of human growth, achievement, and meaningful connections. They encompass essential elements that lead to a well-rounded and prosperous life.

1. Clarity: Discover the power of having a clear vision and purpose that serves as a guiding light through life's uncertainties. When you define your direction, you can navigate challenges with resilience and determination.

2. Proactivity: Become the driver of your destiny by taking responsibility for your actions and decisions. Embrace the mindset that empowers you to shape your future, regardless of external circumstances.

3. Growth Mindset: Unleash the power of your mind by cultivating a growth mindset. Embrace challenges, view failures as stepping stones, and continuously improve to realize your full potential.

4. Effective Communication: Success is often built on meaningful connections. Learn to communicate with empathy, active listening, and assertiveness, thereby fostering enriching relationships that propel you forward.

5. Time Management: Time is the most precious resource at your disposal. Master the art of time management to maximize productivity, achieve balance, and invest your efforts where they matter most.

6. Continuous Learning: In an ever-evolving world, those who keep learning thrive. Develop a hunger for knowledge and a commitment to continuous education, ensuring you remain relevant and adaptable.

7. Empathy and Emotional Intelligence: Recognize the power of emotional intelligence and empathy in nurturing strong connections and creating supportive environments where success can flourish.

Your Path to Elevate Your Life

Throughout this book, you will not only gain insight into these principles but also acquire practical strategies to incorporate them into your daily life. This is not just a book to read; it's a journey of self-discovery and growth.

By the time you turn the last page, you will be equipped with the tools and mindset needed to elevate your life. You will have the clarity to chart your course, the courage to overcome obstacles, and the compassion to inspire and uplift others along the way.

So, I invite you to dive into the 7 core principles of success and embrace this transformational journey. Unleash your potential, embrace the power within, and witness how elevating your life can lead to a profound impact on the world around you. The time to elevate your life is now; the possibilities are limitless. Let us begin!

Chapter 1

The Principle of Clarity

Success begins with clarity - a clear understanding of who you are, what you want, and how you will achieve it. In this chapter, we embark on a profound journey of self-discovery to unlock the power of purpose and vision.

Discovering Your Purpose

The morning sun peeked over the horizon, casting a warm glow on the world below. Emily, a young professional, sat by the window, gazing at the dawning day. Her heart was filled with a sense of longing, a yearning for something more meaningful in her life. She knew she had the potential for greatness, but she couldn't quite put her finger on what that greatness looked like.

In the midst of her contemplation, a question echoed in her mind: "What is my purpose?"

Purpose, that elusive concept that ignites the flames of passion and gives direction to our lives. It is the compass that guides us through the storms of uncertainty and propels us towards our true north.

But for Emily, like many others, the path to purpose seemed shrouded in mist.

Feeling a sense of urgency, Emily decided it was time to embark on a journey of self-discovery. She wanted to find her purpose, to unlock the key that would set her life ablaze with meaning and fulfillment.

As she delved into this exploration, she discovered the first principle of success: clarity. Clarity was the lantern that would pierce through the darkness of confusion and illuminate her purpose.

Discovering her purpose began with introspection. Emily took the time to reflect on her passions, her strengths, and the moments in her life that brought her the most joy. She examined the experiences that resonated with her deeply, and the activities that made her feel most alive.

The more she delved into this self-exploration, the more a pattern emerged. She realized that she felt most fulfilled when she was helping others, using her creativity to solve problems, and making a positive impact on the lives of those around her. It became evident that her purpose lay in making a difference through her unique gifts and talents.

Defining Your Vision

With newfound clarity about her purpose, Emily felt a surge of energy within her. But she knew that clarity alone was not enough. To turn her purpose into reality, she needed a clear vision - a guiding star that would chart the course of her life.

Defining her vision required Emily to dream big and imagine a life beyond her current circumstances. She asked herself, "What would my ideal life look like? What kind of impact do I want to make on the world?"

As she visualized her future, the pieces started falling into place. She saw herself leading a team of passionate individuals, working together to create innovative solutions for societal challenges. She imagined herself standing on stage, sharing her ideas and inspiring others to pursue their dreams.

Her vision became a tapestry of vivid images, emotions, and aspirations. It was a vision that excited her to her core, and she knew she had found her true north.

Aligning Actions with Values

With clarity of purpose and a compelling vision, Emily was ready to set her plans into motion. But she understood that success required more than just lofty dreams; it demanded alignment between her actions and her core values.

She asked herself, "What principles do I hold dear? How do I want to show up in the world? What kind of legacy do I want to leave behind?"

In this introspection, Emily identified her core values - integrity, compassion, and innovation. These values would serve as the foundation upon which she would build her life.

She resolved to make decisions that aligned with her values, even when faced with difficult choices. She knew that staying true to her principles would lead to a life of authenticity and fulfillment.

Cultivating Focus and Direction

As Emily began her journey with purpose, vision, and aligned values, she realized that the path ahead would not always be smooth. Distractions and doubts would undoubtedly emerge, threatening to veer her off course.

Cultivating focus and direction was essential to staying on track. She committed to setting clear and achievable goals that aligned with her vision. She created a roadmap for her personal and professional growth, breaking down her larger vision into smaller, manageable steps.

In times of doubt or uncertainty, she reminded herself of her purpose and vision. Each step she took brought her closer to the life she aspired to live. Her focus sharpened, and her determination grew stronger.

As Emily concluded the first chapter of her journey, she felt an overwhelming sense of gratitude. Clarity had given her a compass, guiding her through the maze of life. Purpose and vision had ignited a fire within her soul. Aligned actions and focus had set her on a path of intention and progress.

With a heart full of hope and excitement, she looked ahead to the next chapter of her life, eager to embrace the challenges and opportunities that lay ahead. Clarity was just the beginning, but it had set her on a course of transformation and elevation.

And so, Emily's journey continued, guided by the first principle of success - the principle of clarity. Little did she know that the discoveries she made in this chapter would be the catalyst for the extraordinary life that awaited her.

Embracing the Path of Exploration

As Emily continued her journey of clarity, she realized that the pursuit of purpose and vision was not a one-time revelation but a lifelong exploration. Clarity was not a destination; it was a journey of self-discovery and evolution.

She embraced the path of exploration with open arms, knowing that as she grew and evolved, her purpose and vision might also transform. She understood that it was okay to revise her goals and aspirations as she gained new insights and experiences.

With this mindset, she embraced the beauty of uncertainty and the joy of discovery. Each day became an opportunity to learn more about herself, to delve deeper into her passions, and to refine her vision.

Overcoming Obstacles and Doubts

Clarity was a powerful force, but Emily knew that the journey would not be without its share of obstacles and doubts. She braced herself for moments of uncertainty and fear, knowing that they were natural parts of the process.

When doubts crept in, she reminded herself of the progress she had already made. She looked back at the moments of clarity, purpose, and vision that had guided her thus far. With renewed determination, she pushed through the challenges, knowing that the path to success was not always a smooth one.

In moments of difficulty, she sought support from those who believed in her and shared her vision. Surrounding herself with positive and encouraging individuals lifted her spirits and reinforced her commitment to her journey.

Celebrating Milestones of Growth

As Emily continued on her journey of clarity, she celebrated every milestone of growth. Each step forward was a victory - a testament to her determination and dedication.

She recognized that success was not solely about reaching the final destination but about cherishing the progress made along the way. Celebrating the small wins fueled her motivation and propelled her further on her path.

With each milestone, she gained a deeper sense of self-confidence and belief in her abilities. The clarity she had found at the beginning of her journey was now ingrained in her heart and soul.

Sharing Clarity and Inspiring Others

As Emily's journey of clarity continued, she became a beacon of inspiration for those around her. Her passion and purpose were infectious, and she shared her experiences with others, encouraging them to embark on their journeys of self-discovery.

She realized that clarity was not meant to be hoarded but to be shared. By inspiring others to find their purpose and vision, she created a ripple effect of positive change in the world.

With every conversation she had, she ignited sparks of possibility in the hearts of those she encountered. She saw the potential for greatness in others, just as she had discovered it within herself.

Conclusion of Chapter 1

As Emily concluded the first chapter of her journey, she felt a sense of awe at the power of clarity. It had transformed her life in ways she could never have imagined. She was no longer a bystander in her own life; she was the architect of her destiny.

With clarity as her compass, Emily knew that she was on the right path. She understood that the journey ahead would be filled with adventure, challenges, and growth, but she welcomed it all with open arms.

Her journey of clarity was just the beginning, but it had set her on a course of purpose and vision. As she turned the page to the next chapter, she looked ahead with excitement and determination.

The journey continued, and Emily was ready to embrace it wholeheartedly. Clarity had unlocked the door to her true potential, and she was eager to explore the boundless possibilities that lay ahead.

Chapter 2

The Principle of Proactivity

Armed with clarity and a strong sense of purpose, we now delve into the empowering principle of proactivity - the key to taking charge of your life and transforming your dreams into reality.

Taking Charge of Your Life

As Emily turned the page to the next chapter of her journey, she knew that the principle of proactivity would be her guiding force. She understood that she held the power to shape her life and that waiting for opportunities to come her way was not enough.

Proactivity meant taking charge of her life and being the author of her destiny. It meant acknowledging that she had the ability to influence the direction of her journey through her actions and choices.

With this newfound perspective, Emily took the reins of her life firmly in her hands. She no longer waited for the perfect moment or external validation to pursue her dreams. Instead, she made a commitment to act with intention and purpose, each step taking her closer to her vision.

Embracing Responsibility

Proactivity also meant embracing responsibility for her decisions and their consequences. Emily understood that the path to success was not without its share of challenges and setbacks. But she also knew that how she responded to those challenges was within her control.

She embraced responsibility as an opportunity to learn and grow, rather than a burden to bear. Each setback became a chance for self-reflection and course correction. Instead of dwelling on what went wrong, she focused on finding solutions and moving forward.

Navigating Adversity with Resilience

As Emily ventured further on her journey of proactivity, she encountered moments of adversity that tested her determination. But proactivity had equipped her with a powerful tool - resilience.

Resilience was the ability to bounce back stronger from setbacks, to persevere in the face of adversity, and to remain steadfast in pursuit of her goals.

In times of difficulty, Emily drew on her inner strength and resilience. She reminded herself of her purpose and vision, and she refused to let temporary setbacks derail her progress. With resilience as her shield, she weathered the storms and emerged stronger on the other side.

Creating Your Own Opportunities

Proactive individuals do not wait for opportunities to knock, they create their own. Emily realized that success was not solely dependent on luck but on her ability to seize opportunities with confidence and determination.

She embraced a mindset of possibility, seeking out opportunities and taking calculated risks. She understood that sometimes, the biggest opportunities lay hidden in the midst of uncertainty.

With each opportunity she created, Emily felt a sense of empowerment. She was no longer a passive observer of her life; she was a proactive participant, actively shaping her future.

Cultivating a Growth Mindset

In her pursuit of proactivity, Emily understood that her mindset played a crucial role in shaping her actions and outcomes. She discovered the concept of a growth mindset – the belief that her abilities and intelligence could be developed through dedication and hard work.

With a growth mindset, Emily saw failures and challenges not as indications of her limitations but as opportunities for learning and growth. She welcomed feedback and criticism as valuable insights to improve herself. This mindset shift allowed her to approach new endeavors with courage and enthusiasm, knowing that even if she didn't have all the answers at the beginning, she had the potential to learn and improve along the way.

Setting Goals and Taking Action

Proactivity without direction could be aimless. To make the most of her proactive mindset, Emily learned the art of goal setting and taking consistent action. She understood that clear and meaningful goals provided her with a sense of purpose and a roadmap for her journey.

Emily set specific, measurable, achievable, relevant, and time-bound (SMART) goals that aligned with her vision. Each day, she broke down her goals into smaller actionable steps and created a plan to achieve them. Through steady progress, she built momentum and celebrated her achievements along the way.

Overcoming Procrastination and Indecision

Procrastination and indecision were formidable adversaries to proactivity. Emily recognized that succumbing to these tendencies could sabotage her progress and lead to missed opportunities.

To overcome procrastination, she practiced self-discipline and time management. Emily established routines and rituals to maintain focus and stay on track with her goals. When faced with indecision, she embraced the principle of experimentation and risk-taking. She accepted that some decisions might not always yield the desired results, but they provided valuable learning experiences.

Inspiring Others through Proactivity

As Emily embodied the principle of proactivity, she noticed a profound impact on those around her. Her proactive approach inspired others to take charge of their lives and pursue their aspirations.

She became a role model for her family, friends, and colleagues, showing them that they, too, possessed the power to create positive change in their lives. Through her actions and attitude, Emily nurtured a culture of proactivity, where individuals felt empowered to make a difference in their personal and professional spheres.

Embracing Adaptability and Flexibility

As Emily continued her journey of proactivity, she encountered the ever-changing landscape of life. She realized that being proactive also meant being adaptable and flexible in the face of unexpected challenges and opportunities.

Emily understood that life was unpredictable, and circumstances could shift in an instant. To thrive in this dynamic environment, she embraced adaptability. She approached change as an invitation to grow and innovate rather than a cause for fear or resistance.

With an open mind and a willingness to learn, Emily navigated through uncertainties with grace and composure. She saw every change as a chance to pivot, evolve, and steer her course towards new horizons.

Building Resilience Through Proactivity

As she embraced adaptability, Emily also discovered that proactivity was instrumental in building her resilience. By taking charge of her life and making proactive decisions, she gained a deeper understanding of her capabilities and strengths.

Each proactive step she took, even in the face of challenges, contributed to her reservoir of resilience. Emily knew that resilience was not about avoiding difficulties but about bouncing back stronger after facing them.

Through proactivity, she learned to embrace setbacks as opportunities for growth. This shift in perspective empowered her to turn obstacles into stepping stones and emerge from difficult situations with newfound wisdom and strength.

Inspiring a Culture of Proactivity

As Emily's journey of proactivity unfolded, she recognized the impact of her actions on her immediate surroundings and beyond. She realized that her proactive approach had the potential to influence not just individuals but entire communities and organizations.

Emily aspired to inspire a culture of proactivity wherever she went. She shared her experiences, knowledge, and insights, encouraging others to take the reins of their lives and pursue their dreams with determination and courage.

By becoming an advocate for proactivity, Emily hoped to ignite a ripple effect of positive change. She believed that when individuals came together with a proactive mindset, they could collectively create a brighter and more fulfilling future.

Embracing Proactivity as a Lifestyle

Proactivity had become more than just a principle for Emily; it had become a way of life. It influenced her daily habits, thoughts, and interactions with others. She saw each day as an opportunity to take purposeful action and move closer to her vision.

Emily embraced the idea that proactivity was not a destination but an ongoing journey. She knew that elevating her life required consistent effort and a commitment to growth.

She found joy in the process of proactivity, knowing that every step she took aligned with her values and aspirations. This proactive approach allowed her to savor each moment and find fulfillment in the pursuit of her dreams.

Proactivity and the Ripple Effect

As Emily's proactive approach continued to shape her life, she began to witness the ripple effect of her actions on those around her. Her proactive mindset and attitude inspired others to take charge of their own lives and pursue their goals with renewed vigor.

In her workplace, colleagues noticed Emily's proactive approach to problem-solving and decision-making. They admired her ability to take initiative and lead by example. As a result, the team became more proactive as a whole, fostering a culture of continuous improvement and innovation.

Within her family, Emily's proactivity influenced her loved ones to adopt a more intentional and purpose-driven approach to their lives. They recognized the power of taking responsibility for their actions and embracing change as a catalyst for growth.

Overcoming Obstacles with Proactivity

Proactivity did not shield Emily from encountering obstacles; rather, it armed her with the resilience and determination needed to overcome them. When faced with challenges, she refused to be deterred and used her proactive mindset to seek solutions.

Rather than becoming paralyzed by fear or uncertainty, Emily channeled her energy into proactively addressing the issues at hand. She sought support and guidance when needed, and her willingness to take action inspired others to rally around her.

Cultivating a Proactive Lifestyle

For Emily, proactivity was more than a single trait or decision; it was a lifestyle she had embraced wholeheartedly. Each day presented opportunities for growth and progress, and she approached them with intention and enthusiasm.

She incorporated proactive habits into her daily routine, such as setting aside time for reflection and goal-setting, seeking feedback to enhance her performance, and making time for learning and personal development.

With a proactive lifestyle, Emily found that she was better equipped to manage stress and uncertainty. Instead of being reactive and overwhelmed, she remained focused on her vision and calmly navigated through challenges.

Proactivity and Gratitude

Gratitude was another essential element of Emily's proactive journey. She acknowledged the abundance of opportunities and resources available to her, and she was grateful for the lessons learned from both successes and setbacks.

Emily practiced gratitude not only for her own blessings but for the contributions and support of those who had helped her along the way. Expressing gratitude nurtured her relationships and deepened the sense of community around her.

Conclusion of Chapter 2

As Emily concluded her exploration of the Principle of Proactivity, she felt a sense of empowerment and purpose coursing through her being. This principle had ignited a transformative fire within her, illuminating the path to a life of intention, action, and self-determination.

Through the lens of proactivity, Emily had come to understand that her life was not a passive experience but a canvas waiting for her artistic touch. She had grasped the reins of her destiny and embraced her role as the captain of her own ship.

With a firm grasp on the wheel, Emily navigated through the vast sea of possibilities, unafraid of the challenges that lay ahead. She knew that obstacles were not roadblocks but stepping stones, propelling her towards growth and accomplishment.

Emily's journey through proactivity had taught her that waiting for circumstances to align was a fleeting strategy. Instead, she had harnessed the power of her choices, shaping her destiny one proactive step at a time.

In embracing responsibility, Emily had not only accepted the power to influence her own life but had become a source of inspiration for others. Her proactive approach had kindled a spark in those around her, encouraging them to take ownership of their actions and destinies.

Resilience had become her loyal companion, bolstering her spirit in the face of adversity. Emily had learned that setbacks were not defeats but moments of refinement, molding her into a stronger and more resilient individual.

The art of creating her own opportunities had opened doors she hadn't even known existed. By daring to step beyond her comfort zone, Emily had discovered new realms of possibility and accomplishment.

Emily's journey through the Principle of Proactivity was a testament to the transformative power of taking charge of one's life. With each proactive choice, she had woven a tapestry of intention and purpose, crafting a life that resonated with authenticity and fulfillment.

As she turned the page to the next chapter, Emily carried with her the essence of proactivity—a driving force that would continue to shape her journey of elevation. She felt a renewed determination to seize the reins of her life, to embrace challenges with resilience, and to create opportunities that aligned with her vision.

And so, with a heart full of purpose and a mind set on action, Emily ventured forth into the uncharted territory of the next chapter, ready to embrace the principles that would further elevate her life.

Chapter 3

The Principle of Growth Mindset

As we venture into the realm of personal growth and development, we encounter the transformative principle of a growth mindset. This chapter delves into the power of our beliefs and how adopting a growth-oriented mindset can revolutionize our approach to challenges and opportunities.

Understanding Fixed vs. Growth Mindset

As Emily ventured into the next phase of her journey, she encountered the transformative principle of a growth mindset. She realized that her beliefs about her abilities could profoundly impact her actions and, consequently, her outcomes.

She learned that individuals with a fixed mindset believed that their talents and intelligence were innate and unchangeable. On the other hand, those with a growth mindset believed that their abilities could be developed through dedication, effort, and continuous learning.

Emily understood the significance of cultivating a growth mindset. By embracing the belief that she could learn and improve, she freed herself from the limitations of a fixed mindset and opened herself up to a world of possibilities.

Embracing Challenges as Opportunities

With her newfound growth mindset, Emily began to view challenges through a different lens. Rather than shying away from difficulties, she saw them as opportunities for growth and learning.

She welcomed challenges with a sense of excitement and curiosity, knowing that they presented chances to stretch her abilities and expand her horizons.

In each challenge, Emily discovered the power of perseverance and resilience. Instead of giving up when faced with obstacles, she pushed through, knowing that her efforts were not in vain.

The Power of Yet: Turning Failures into Stepping Stones

Failures were no longer crushing blows to Emily's confidence; they became stepping stones on her path to success. With her growth mindset, she embraced the idea of "the power of yet."

When faced with a setback or failure, Emily reframed her thinking. Instead of thinking, "I can't do this," she replaced it with, "I can't do this yet, but with effort and practice, I will improve."

This shift in perspective allowed her to view failures as temporary setbacks rather than permanent defeats. With each failure, she gleaned valuable insights and learned to course-correct on her journey to greatness.

Continuously Improving Yourself

The growth mindset instilled in Emily a hunger for continuous improvement. She realized that the journey to success was not a one-time destination but a constant evolution.

She set out on a path of lifelong learning, seeking out opportunities to expand her knowledge and skills. She read books, attended workshops, and sought feedback from mentors and peers.

With each new piece of knowledge she acquired, Emily felt herself growing stronger and more capable. She understood that improvement was not a linear process; it was about embracing the ups and downs of the learning curve.

Embracing Feedback and Criticism

Within the realm of the growth mindset, Emily recognized the importance of feedback and criticism as tools for growth. She understood that receiving constructive input from others was an opportunity to enhance her skills and refine her approach.

Emily embraced feedback with an open heart, seeking to extract valuable insights that would propel her forward. Instead of perceiving criticism as a personal attack, she viewed it as a chance to improve and evolve.

She learned to differentiate between feedback that was constructive and that which was detrimental, using her discernment to sift through opinions and integrate the ones that resonated with her goals.

Cultivating Resilience through Mindset

Resilience became a defining trait of Emily's growth mindset journey. She discovered that her mindset played a pivotal role in her ability to bounce back from setbacks and navigate through adversity.

When faced with challenges that tested her resolve, Emily tapped into the power of her growth mindset. She reminded herself that setbacks were not indicators of her worth or potential; rather, they were stepping stones on the path to her aspirations.

Through resilience, Emily harnessed the strength to persevere, even in the face of seemingly insurmountable obstacles. Her growth mindset served as a wellspring of courage and determination, propelling her forward with unwavering resolve.

Spreading the Seeds of Growth

As Emily continued to cultivate her growth mindset, she recognized the impact it had on those around her. Her friends, family, and colleagues witnessed her transformation and were inspired by her journey of self-discovery and improvement.

Emily became an advocate for the growth mindset, sharing her experiences and insights with others. She encouraged them to challenge their fixed beliefs, embrace failures as opportunities, and adopt a mindset of continuous improvement.

Through her actions and words, Emily planted seeds of growth in the hearts and minds of those she touched. She saw how her journey inspired others to embark on their own quests for self-improvement, fostering a culture of growth and development.

Conclusion of Chapter 3

As Emily reached the conclusion of her exploration into the Principle of Growth Mindset, she stood at the precipice of a profound transformation. This principle had reshaped her perception of challenges, failures, and her own potential, propelling her towards a path of boundless growth and self-discovery.

The understanding that her beliefs were not fixed, but rather malleable and adaptable, had liberated Emily from the confines of a limited mindset. She had witnessed how embracing a growth mindset had enabled her to approach challenges with curiosity, view failures as stepping stones, and persist with unwavering determination.

Through the power of "yet," Emily had reframed her internal dialogue, turning self-doubt into a catalyst for progress. The notion that she hadn't achieved something "yet" had become a mantra of possibility, fuelling her drive to continuously improve and evolve.

Emily's journey through the Principle of Growth Mindset had been marked by the cultivation of resilience. She had discovered that setbacks were not roadblocks, but rather opportunities to display the strength of her spirit and bounce back even stronger.

With every step, Emily had become a living embodiment of the growth mindset. Her thirst for knowledge had driven her to seek out learning opportunities, adapting to the ebb and flow of the learning curve with grace and determination.

Moreover, Emily's growth had extended beyond herself. Her transformation had radiated outward, inspiring those around her to embark on their own journeys of self-improvement. By embodying the principles of a growth mindset, Emily had sowed seeds of possibility and change, contributing to the growth of her community.

As Emily looked back on her exploration of the growth mindset, she felt a sense of empowerment unlike anything she had experienced before. The shackles of self-doubt had been replaced by wings of aspiration, carrying her higher and farther than she had ever imagined.

With the principles of growth, resilience, and continuous improvement as her companions, Emily felt a surge of confidence. As she turned the page to the next chapter, the Principle of Time Management beckoned, promising to equip her with the tools to make the most of every moment and further propel her towards her vision.

Chapter 4

The Principle of Effective Communication

In this pivotal chapter, we shift our focus to the realm of interpersonal relationships and communication - the lifeblood of success in both personal and professional spheres. Effective communication forms the bedrock of strong connections, collaboration, and understanding.

The Art of Active Listening

As Emily delved into the realm of interpersonal relationships and communication, she recognized the importance of active listening. Communication was not just about speaking, it was equally about truly hearing and understanding others.

Emily realized that active listening required her full presence and attention. She practiced suspending judgment and giving her undivided focus to the person speaking.

By honing her active listening skills, Emily discovered that she could forge deeper connections with others. People felt valued and understood when she listened attentively, fostering a sense of trust and openness in her interactions.

Practicing Empathetic Understanding

Empathy was the key to unlocking meaningful connections. Emily understood that true empathy involved putting herself in another person's shoes and seeing the world from their perspective.

In her conversations, Emily practiced empathetic understanding by acknowledging others' emotions and validating their experiences. She learned that empathy was not about solving problems but about offering a supportive presence and a listening ear.

As she embraced empathy, Emily found that her relationships grew stronger and more authentic. She felt a deeper sense of connection with others, and she learned to navigate conflicts with grace and compassion.

Assertive Expression for Positive Impact

Emily recognized that effective communication was a two-way street. While active listening and empathy were essential, she also understood the importance of assertive expression.

Assertiveness meant expressing her thoughts and feelings confidently and respectfully. She learned to communicate her needs, boundaries, and opinions without resorting to aggression or passivity.

By embracing assertive expression, Emily found her voice and felt empowered in her interactions. She realized that effective communication was not just about understanding others but also about being understood herself.

Building Trust and Strong Relationships

At the core of effective communication was trust. Emily knew that trust was the cornerstone of successful relationships, both personal and professional.

She worked diligently to build trust with others by being reliable, honest, and transparent in her interactions. She understood that trust was not earned overnight; it was built through consistent actions and communication.

As Emily fostered trust in her relationships, she saw the positive impact it had on collaboration and teamwork. Trust created a safe space for open communication, creative problem-solving, and collective success.

Conclusion of Chapter 4

As Emily concluded the fourth chapter of her journey, she marveled at the profound impact of effective communication. By practicing active listening, empathy, and assertive expression, she had transformed her interactions with others.

Effective communication was not just a tool for conveying information; it was the key to building bridges of understanding and fostering meaningful connections.

As she turned the page to the next chapter, Emily knew that effective communication would continue to be a guiding principle in her journey to elevate her life. The power of her words and the connections she forged would become her superpower in creating a positive impact on the world.

The journey continued, and Emily was ready to embrace the next chapter with an open heart and a willingness to connect deeply with others.

Chapter 5

The Principle of Time Management

Time, the most valuable resource, demands careful attention and management. In this chapter, we explore the art of time management, a skill that distinguishes successful individuals who maximize their productivity and achieve their goals while maintaining a healthy work-life balance.

The Value of Time as a Finite Resource

As Emily embarked on the next phase of her journey, she encountered the crucial principle of time management. Time, she realized, was the most precious and finite resource she possessed.

She understood that how she utilized her time would directly impact her progress towards her goals and aspirations. With this awareness, Emily resolved to treat each moment with intention and purpose.

No longer would she allow time to slip through her fingers unnoticed. Instead, she would be mindful of how she invested her time, ensuring that it aligned with her vision and values.

Prioritizing Tasks for Maximum Impact

Emily recognized that not all tasks held equal importance in her journey to success. To make the most of her time, she needed to prioritize her tasks based on their significance and urgency.

She adopted strategies such as the Eisenhower Matrix and the 80/20 rule to help her discern which tasks would yield the greatest results. By focusing on high-impact activities, Emily knew she could make progress towards her vision more efficiently.

Minimizing Distractions and Time Wasters

In an age of constant distractions, Emily understood the importance of safeguarding her focus. Time management required her to minimize distractions and time-wasting activities that hindered her productivity.

She created a conducive environment for concentration, eliminating unnecessary interruptions. Emily learned to embrace time blocking, allocating specific periods for focused work and dedicated breaks.

By mindfully managing technology and setting boundaries, she ensured that her time was channeled into meaningful endeavors.

Striking a Work-Life Balance for Well-being

As Emily continued her exploration of time management, she acknowledged the significance of striking a healthy work-life balance. Success, she realized, was not solely about achievements; it encompassed her overall well-being and happiness.

She resolved to prioritize self-care and set aside time for activities that brought her joy and relaxation. Emily knew that maintaining her well-being was essential for sustaining her productivity and enthusiasm on her journey.

Emily's journey into the Principle of Time Management led her to a profound realization: that true success was not solely defined by accomplishments but by a holistic sense of well-being. She understood that her well-being was the foundation upon which her achievements were built.

Emily became intentional about creating a harmonious balance between her work and personal life. She knew that overexerting herself in one area could lead to burnout and hinder her overall progress. With this in mind, she began to implement strategies to foster a healthy equilibrium.

She set clear boundaries for work-related activities, designating specific hours for focused tasks. During her designated breaks, Emily engaged in activities that rejuvenated her, whether it was taking a walk, practicing mindfulness, or spending quality time with loved ones.

By prioritizing self-care, Emily found herself replenished and ready to tackle challenges with renewed vigor. She recognized that a well-rested and fulfilled mind was more productive, creative, and capable of making meaningful contributions.

Conclusion of Chapter 5

As Emily concluded the fifth chapter of her journey, she felt a profound sense of control over her time. Time management had become her ally, empowering her to make deliberate choices and invest in her priorities.

She understood that time was a precious currency that she could spend wisely. By prioritizing tasks, minimizing distractions, and maintaining a work-life balance, Emily knew she was optimizing her time for growth and fulfillment.

As she turned the page to the next chapter, Emily was equipped with the knowledge that time management was not about squeezing more into her day but about aligning her actions with her vision. The principle of time management would continue to be the foundation of her productivity and success.

The journey continued, and Emily was eager to make every moment count on her path to elevate her life.

Chapter 6

The Principle of Continuous Learning

In a rapidly evolving world, the key to staying relevant and thriving is a commitment to continuous learning. This chapter delves into the power of education, curiosity, and adaptability in driving your personal and professional growth.

Embracing a Lifelong Learning Mindset

In a rapidly changing world, Emily realized that the pursuit of knowledge and growth was essential for staying relevant and adaptable. She embraced the principle of continuous learning with enthusiasm, recognizing that curiosity was the key to unlocking new possibilities.

Emily approached each day as an opportunity to learn something new. She sought out books, courses, and workshops that expanded her horizons and enriched her understanding of the world.

With a thirst for knowledge, Emily nurtured a lifelong learning mindset that fueled her curiosity and passion for personal and professional development.

Staying Curious and Adapting to Change

In her journey of continuous learning, Emily discovered that staying curious was the driving force behind her adaptability. Instead of fearing change, she welcomed it as an invitation to grow.

Emily understood that embracing change was not just about survival but about thriving in a dynamic world. With her growth mindset and curiosity as allies, she approached change with an open mind and a willingness to learn.

Learning from Mistakes and Feedback

Emily recognized that mistakes were not failures but valuable learning opportunities. She understood that setbacks were stepping stones on her path to success.

Rather than being disheartened by mistakes, Emily viewed them as chances to grow and improve. She embraced a mindset of continuous improvement and actively sought feedback from others to gain new perspectives and insights.

With each lesson learned, Emily became more resilient and resourceful, armed with the wisdom to navigate challenges with grace.

Innovating and Remaining Relevant

As Emily continued her pursuit of continuous learning, she understood that innovation was the natural outcome of a curious and adaptable mind.

She challenged herself to think creatively and outside the box. Emily explored new ideas and approaches, always looking for ways to improve and make a positive impact.

Innovation became the hallmark of her journey, setting her apart as a trailblazer in her field. With a passion for learning and an innovative spirit, Emily remained relevant and at the forefront of progress.

Emily's embrace of the Principle of Continuous Learning propelled her into a world of innovation and relevance. She recognized that her journey was not just about acquiring knowledge but applying it in transformative ways.

With each new skill she acquired and each insight she gained, Emily sought opportunities to innovate. She looked at challenges from fresh perspectives, unafraid to question conventions and explore uncharted territories.

Innovation became her companion in problem-solving. Emily's commitment to continuous learning allowed her to bring novel solutions to the table, inspiring others and leaving an indelible mark on her endeavors.

Through innovation, Emily remained a dynamic force in her field. Her ability to adapt and evolve made her an invaluable asset to her team, organization, and the broader community.

Conclusion of Chapter 6

As Emily concluded the sixth chapter of her journey, she marveled at the transformative power of continuous learning. It had become the driving force behind her growth and success.

With each step she took on her path of continuous learning, Emily knew that she was not just acquiring knowledge but becoming a better version of herself. Her insatiable curiosity and adaptability were shaping her into a person of immense potential and possibility.

As she turned the page to the next chapter, Emily was ready to embrace the journey of lifelong learning with an open heart and an eager mind. The principle of continuous learning would continue to be her compass, guiding her towards a future filled with endless growth and evolution.

The journey continued, and Emily felt a sense of wonder and excitement at the limitless opportunities that awaited her on her quest to elevate her life.

Chapter 7

The Principle of Empathy and Emotional Intelligence

At the heart of success lies the ability to connect deeply with others, foster strong relationships, and create a supportive environment. This chapter explores the transformative power of empathy and emotional intelligence in nurturing meaningful connections and collective success.

The Role of Empathy in Success

At the heart of success lies the ability to connect deeply with others, foster strong relationships, and create a supportive environment. This chapter explores the transformative power of empathy and emotional intelligence in nurturing meaningful connections and collective success.

Emily understood that empathy was the cornerstone of emotional intelligence and effective communication. She delved into the significance of empathy in understanding the emotions and perspectives of others. By putting herself in others' shoes, Emily discovered how empathy enabled her to connect on a deeper level, cultivate trust, and build a strong support network.

Understanding and Managing Emotions

Emotions are a natural part of the human experience, and emotional intelligence is the ability to understand and manage these emotions effectively. In this section, Emily explored the art of emotional intelligence, empowering her to recognize and regulate her emotions, as well as empathize with the feelings of others.

By mastering emotional intelligence, Emily made wiser decisions and navigated interpersonal dynamics with grace and tact. She learned to respond to challenging situations with composure and empathy, enhancing her effectiveness in personal and professional relationships.

Nurturing Positive and Supportive Environments

Positive environments are conducive to growth and success. In this section, Emily delved into the role of empathy and emotional intelligence in creating supportive spaces that fostered collaboration, creativity, and well-being.

She learned how to cultivate a culture of kindness, respect, and inclusivity, laying the foundation for collective achievement. Emily recognized that a nurturing environment empowered individuals to thrive and contribute their best to shared goals.

Collaboration and Teamwork for Collective Success

Success was not solely an individual pursuit but often a collective endeavor. In this final section, Emily emphasized the power of collaboration and teamwork in achieving ambitious goals.

She explored strategies to build effective teams, leverage diverse perspectives, and work harmoniously towards shared objectives. By cultivating empathy and emotional intelligence within teams, Emily discovered that she could harness the collective potential of each member and achieve extraordinary results.

Conclusion of Chapter 7

As Emily concluded the seventh chapter of her journey, she recognized the immense value of empathy and emotional intelligence in her personal and professional life.

Embracing empathy and emotional intelligence allowed her to create a ripple effect of positive change, touching the lives of those around her. Emily's capacity for empathy and emotional intelligence became the driving force behind her impact on the world.

With a heart filled with compassion and understanding, Emily knew that her journey was not just about elevating her own life but about uplifting others. As she turned the page to the final section of this book, Emily was committed to making empathy and emotional intelligence the guiding principles in her interactions with the world.

The journey continued, and Emily understood that her ability to connect with others and foster a supportive environment would be a source of boundless strength and fulfillment.

And so, the journey continued, and Emily's heart and mind were forever expanded by the principles of empathy and emotional intelligence, guiding her toward a path of deeper understanding and shared success.

Epilogue: A Life Elevated

As Emily reached the end of her transformative journey, she found herself filled with a sense of fulfillment and purpose. The principles she had embraced had become ingrained in her being, guiding her actions, decisions, and relationships.

With empathy as her compass, Emily's perspective on life had shifted. She saw the world through a lens of compassion, understanding that everyone she encountered carried their own joys, struggles, and aspirations.

Her emotional intelligence had grown immensely, allowing her to navigate the complexities of human interactions with grace and wisdom. Emily had learned to respond, not react, to the challenges that came her way. She approached difficult conversations with empathy, seeking mutual understanding and resolution.

In nurturing positive environments, Emily had become a beacon of support for her friends, family, and colleagues. By creating a space where people felt seen, heard, and valued, she had become a catalyst for growth and collaboration.

In the realm of collaboration and teamwork, Emily had discovered the beauty of collective effort. She embraced diverse perspectives, knowing that they enriched the collective wisdom of any group. As a team player, Emily appreciated the strengths of others and was always ready to offer her support and encouragement.

Emily's journey of elevation had not been without its share of challenges and setbacks. But she had learned that each obstacle was an opportunity to practice the principles she had embraced. With a growth mindset, she saw failures not as dead-ends, but as stepping stones towards progress.

As she reflected on her transformation, Emily realized that elevating her life was not a destination but a continuous journey. The principles she had learned were not finite milestones but guiding stars, illuminating the path ahead.

Her life had become a canvas of growth, empathy, and meaningful connections. And as she continued her journey, she knew that the principles she had embraced would continue to shape her destiny.

The story of Emily's elevation was not just a personal tale, but an invitation for others to embark on their own transformative journey. Through the pages of this book, she hoped to inspire others to discover their purpose, embrace proactivity, cultivate a growth mindset, communicate effectively, manage time wisely, pursue continuous learning, and lead with empathy and emotional intelligence.

For, in the end, the journey to elevate one's life was not a solo endeavor but a collective quest for a better, brighter world. As each individual embraced these core principles of success, the ripple of positive change would spread far and wide, transcending boundaries and touching hearts.

And so, as the final chapter came to a close, Emily knew that her journey of elevation had only just begun. With boundless curiosity, resilience, and compassion, she looked ahead to the infinite possibilities that lay before her.

And as she turned the last page of this book, she felt the gentle whisper of life's greatest truth - that the journey of elevation was not just about reaching the summit, but about savoring every step along the way.

For it was in the pursuit of growth, connection, and purpose that life revealed its true beauty. And in each moment lived with intention and heart, Emily found herself truly elevated - not just in success, but in the very essence of being human.

Embracing the Seven Core Principles

As Emily completed the 7 core principles of success, she reflected on the profound changes they had brought into her life. Each principle had become a guiding light, illuminating her path and empowering her to elevate every aspect of her being.

Through the principle of clarity, Emily had discovered her purpose and set her sights on a compelling vision for her future. The principle of proactivity had empowered her to take charge of her life, embrace responsibility, and create her own opportunities.

With a growth mindset, Emily had embraced challenges as stepping stones and continuous learning as the key to personal development. Effective communication had strengthened her relationships and fostered a culture of empathy and understanding.

By mastering time management, Emily had found balance and efficiency, making the most of each precious moment. The principle of continuous learning had fueled her curiosity and kept her agile in the face of change.

Finally, the principle of empathy and emotional intelligence had deepened her connections with others and inspired collaborative efforts for collective success.

As Emily looked back on her journey, she realized that elevating her life was not an end goal but an ever-evolving process. Each principle represented a thread interwoven into the tapestry of her life, forming a beautiful and intricate pattern of growth and transformation.

She knew that the journey of elevation was not without challenges, setbacks, and uncertainties. Yet, armed with the 7 core principles of success, Emily had embraced life with open arms, knowing that every experience presented an opportunity for growth and self-discovery.

As she continued her journey, Emily held in her heart a deep sense of gratitude for the lessons learned and the people who had touched her life along the way. She understood that true success was not just about personal achievements but about uplifting others and making a positive impact on the world.

Through her proactive approach, Emily had not only elevated her own life but had become a beacon of inspiration for those around her. She had sown seeds of possibility and hope, igniting the potential for greatness in others.

And so, as Emily turned the final page of this transformative journey, she knew that her story was not an isolated tale but an invitation for others to embark on their own journey of elevation. She hoped that the 7 core principles of success would serve as a compass for others, guiding them towards a life of purpose, fulfillment, and boundless potential.

With a heart filled with gratitude, passion, and a commitment to growth, Emily stepped forward into the vast horizon of possibilities that awaited her. The journey of elevation continued, and she was ready to embrace every moment with intention, courage, and love.

And so, dear reader, may this book be your guiding light as you embark on your own journey of elevation. Embrace the 7 core principles of success, and let them lead you towards a life of purpose, impact, and fulfillment.

Remember, you hold the power to elevate your life and make a difference in the world. Embrace each day with a proactive spirit, and let the journey of elevation be the masterpiece of your life.

Reflecting on your journey

Dear reader as you completed "Elevate Your Life: The 7 Core Principles of Success," take a moment to reflect on the transformative journey you have embarked upon. The seven core principles of clarity, proactivity, growth mindset, effective communication, time management, continuous learning, empathy, and emotional intelligence are now woven into the fabric of your being.

You are now equipped with the tools, knowledge, and wisdom to elevate your life and make a profound impact on the world around you. Embrace the clarity of your purpose, the proactivity of your actions, the growth mindset of continuous improvement, the power of effective communication, the efficiency of time management, the thirst for knowledge and adaptability, the warmth of empathy, and the wisdom of emotional intelligence.

Remember that success is not a destination but an ongoing journey of growth and contribution. As you continue your quest for excellence, be patient with yourself and kind to others. Celebrate your victories, learn from your setbacks, and never stop pursuing your dreams.

With each step, you inch closer to the extraordinary life you deserve. Embrace the challenges, savor the moments of triumph, and above all, cherish the connections you forge along the way. You are the author of your story, and the world is your canvas. Go forth, and elevate your life to new heights of success and fulfillment. The journey never ends, and the best is yet to come.

This is not the end; it is just the beginning of a life elevated - a life of purpose, passion, and boundless possibilities. As you embark on the next chapter of your journey, go forth with confidence, knowing that you possess the keys to unlock the extraordinary life that awaits you.

Elevate your life, and let your light shine brightly in the world.

The journey continues, and the best is yet to come.

And so, dear reader, let your journey of elevation begin.

The journey continues.......................

Author's Thank You Message

Dear Reader,

As you reach the final pages of "Elevate Your Life: The 7 Core Principles of Success," I want to extend my heartfelt gratitude to you. Thank you for embarking on this journey of growth and transformation with me.

Your commitment to learning, your dedication to self-improvement, and your willingness to embrace change are truly inspiring. It is my sincere hope that the principles shared within these chapters have ignited a spark of positive change in your life.

Remember, success is not a solitary endeavor; it's a collective journey. Your journey towards elevation is a testament to your resilience and determination. Each step you take, each principle you apply, brings you closer to the life you envision.

I encourage you to continue applying these principles, to keep striving for your goals, and to never underestimate the incredible potential that resides within you. Your journey of elevation has only just begun, and I am honored to have been a part of it.

Thank you for entrusting me with your time and attention. May your path be filled with purpose, growth, and the fulfillment of your dreams.

With heartfelt thanks,

Tony Oloko

Author

Made in the USA
Columbia, SC
27 November 2023